BIBLE
DOCTRINES

◆

– Part 1 –

R. E.
HARLOW

LUKE 24:27

Developed as a study course by Emmaus Correspondence School, founded in 1942.

Many Bible study courses may also be taken via smart phones, tablets, and computers. For more information, visit the ECS website www.ecsministries.org.

Bible Doctrines — Part 1
R. E. Harlow

Published by:

Emmaus Correspondence School
(A division of ECS Ministries)
P.O. Box 1028
Dubuque, IA 52004-1028
phone: (563) 585-2070
email: ecsorders@ecsministries.org
website: www.ecsministries.org

First Edition 2016 (AK '16), 2 UNITS

ISBN 978-1-59387-240-3

Code: BD1

Copyright © 2016 ECS Ministries

Previously published as part of *Basic Bible Doctrines*, copyright © 1968, 1972, 2005 by R. E. Harlow, published by ECS Ministries.

Printed in the United States of America

STUDENT INSTRUCTIONS

66 "All Scripture . . . is profitable for doctrine . . ." (2 Timothy 3:16). This 2-part course will guide you through a topical study of the major teachings (doctrines) of Scripture, referencing many relevant verses and passages relating to each doctrine. With an open Bible and an open heart, you will indeed profit from learning what the Scripture teaches about itself, God, Jesus Christ, and the Holy Spirit in Part 1, and angels, man, sin, salvation, the church, and future events in Part 2.

LESSONS YOU WILL STUDY

Note: *Bible Doctrines – Part 2* covers Angelology, Anthropology, Hamartiology, Soteriology, Ecclesiology, and Eschatology.

Course Components

This course has two parts: this study course and the exam booklet.

How To Study

This study has eight chapters, and each chapter has its own exam. Begin by asking God to help you understand the material. Read the chapter through at least twice, once to get a general idea of its contents and then again, slowly, looking up any Bible references given.

Begin studying immediately, or if you are in a group, as soon as the group begins. We suggest that you keep a regular schedule by trying to complete at least one chapter per week.

Exams

In the exam booklet there is one exam for each chapter (exam 1 covers chapter 1 of the course). Do not answer the questions by what you think or have always believed. The questions are designed to find out if you understand the material given in the course.

After you have completed each chapter, review the related exam and see how well you know the answers. If you find that you are having difficulty answering the questions, review the material until you think you can answer the questions. It is important that you read the Bible passages referenced as some questions may be based on the Bible text.

How Your Exams Are Graded

Your instructor will mark any incorrectly answered questions. You will be referred back to the place in the course where the correct answer is to be found. After finishing this course with a passing average, you will be awarded a certificate.

If you enrolled in a class, submit your exam papers to the leader or secretary of the class who will send them for the entire group to the Correspondence School.

See the back of the exam booklet for more information on returning the exams for grading.

1

BIBLIOLOGY: THE STUDY OF THE BIBLE – PART 1 –

The Bible claims to be a revelation from God about Himself. The study of what the Bible teaches about itself is called *Bibliology*.

The Concept of Revelation

Human philosophy is an attempt to understand the nature of the universe. While this in itself is a noble desire, it usually starts with the avowed purpose of eliminating the need for a revelation from a Creator, a Supreme Being to whom we human beings are responsible. Thus it turns out to be a series of self-canceling theories.

> **Any definition of God which denies His supernatural power is a contradiction in terms.**

We will begin with the premise that man *is* a created being, and that our Creator has the *ability* to reveal Himself. Any definition of God which denies His supernatural power is a contradiction in terms; He would not be God if He did not have such power. Building on from that thought, it is logical to assume that as we humans can reveal our minds to other humans (and to a lesser degree, even to animals), our Creator could reveal Himself to man if He wanted to. The question then is: *Why* would He want to?

In answer, it is reasonable to conclude that if God expects His creatures to know what He expects of them, He would have to reveal His will to them. Otherwise, how could He hold them responsible for disobeying Him? Another reason relates to His personal nature: Why would He create a race of intelligent beings unless it was His desire and plan to reveal Himself to them and relate to them in a mutually beneficial and enjoyable way?

The next logical question is, is *the Bible* God's revelation of Himself? Some books that are held sacred by their followers (such as the *Koran* and the *Book of Mormon*) claim to be revelations from the one true God. The Bible claims to be the one and only revelation from God and, on the basis of evidence alone, is incomparably more likely to be so than any other religious book in existence. (The ECS course *God's Word Is Truth* is a good resource on this topic.) Consider a few lines of evidence now.

The Unity of the Bible

To begin with, there is *the unity of the Bible*. Imagine a single book today in which some parts were written in the year AD 500, others around 1000, many about 1200 to 1500, then after a gap of 400 years, another whole set of very important volumes being written and added to the collection around the year 1900. Reason dictates that they would all be different and contradictory. The 66 books in the Bible were penned by about 40 different men from different walks of life (kings, shepherds, preachers, farmers, priests, a doctor, and others) over a similar period of time (about 1500 years, from about 1400 BC to AD 100). Yet although they differ greatly in nature, style, and content, they unify around one broad theme: the person of God's Son, the Lord Jesus Christ, and the history of His redeeming man from sin.

Ancient History

Another facet that supports the Bible's claim to be a divine revelation is *ancient history*. Reliable secular history of the ancient world invariably supports what is recorded in the Bible. Archaeologists dig around the ruins of ancient cities and find records that help them understand ancient history. At first, some of these records seem to disagree with the Bible, and too often it is assumed that the Bible must be wrong and the ancient historian correct. The trend in recent years, however, even among secular historians, has been to substantiate the Bible as historically accurate after all.

Miracles

Many objections to the historical accuracy of the Bible are based on the preconceived idea that *miracles* are impossible. Every thoughtful person, however, would have to concede that if there truly is a God, He not only *could* be expected to act in a supernatural manner, but *would*.

Fulfilled Prophecy

Another proof that God has revealed Himself in the book we call the Bible is found in *fulfilled biblical prophecy*. Centuries before Jesus Christ came, the prophets of God foretold when, where, and how He would be born, and that He would die and rise again. Many details prophesied in the Old Testament are seen to be fulfilled in the New Testament. Only God could have supplied this kind of specific knowledge centuries ahead of time. Unbelievers try to get around this remarkable proof by saying that the prophecies were written after the events had taken place. But a careful study will show that such a charge is inadequate and false.

The Bible's Power to Convict

Another remarkable fact about the Bible is its *convicting power*—its ability to make people feel guilty of sin. The Old Testament gives God's holy Law, which no mere man has ever kept perfectly. The New Testament records the life of the perfect God-man, the Lord Jesus Christ. If anyone thinks he can keep God's Law, Jesus must be his standard. Millions reading the Bible realize their own failure and feel condemned before God.

The Bible's Life-Transforming Power

The *life-transforming power* of the Bible is another proof of its divine origin. We could have no peace or joy if the Bible merely left us feeling condemned. This, however, is only the preparation for the message of salvation. The Bible tells us of a Savior so wonderful that no one in any other book in the world can compare with Him. Basically, every religious book tells what man has to do to live forever or to please the deity he or she fears and worships. Only Christianity proclaims that eternal life is the gracious gift of God for the one who believes in Christ. Christ has paid the penalty of sin, and there is nothing left to do on man's part but to believe it and embrace it. God's plan of salvation is much too wonderful, too simple, and too beautiful to be the work of mere man. Many lives have been completely changed through the message of Christ. Untold millions—rich and poor, religious and worldly, heathen and agnostic—have found peace through the Bible's most important message.

> The Bible tells us of a Savior so wonderful that no one in any other book in the world can compare with Him.

Endurance and Preservation of the Bible

The *enduring value and preservation* of the Bible is one more proof of its divine character. Some people reject the Bible because it is old. Yet the very fact that the Bible *is* so ancient is important. God has preserved it through the centuries. Of course, other ancient books have survived the centuries as well. However, none of them has been required to miraculously survive numerous bitter attempts to destroy it as has the Bible. God has kept it for us until now because it is His recorded message to mankind.

> Any open-minded person can turn to the Bible and expect to hear the voice of God speaking to him or her through it.

And what about today? If, as some people say, the Bible is so out-of-date, and if, as some scientists have stated, the Bible is full of error, we might assume that it is no longer wanted. Yet the Bible continues to be the Number One best-selling book in the world. At least a part of the Bible has been translated into over 2,000 languages or dialects, and the majority of the world's population can understand one or more of these languages. Many millions of Bibles have been printed.

For these reasons and others, any open-minded person can turn to the Bible and expect to hear the voice of God speaking to him or her through it.

The Doctrine of Inspiration

In 2 Timothy 3:16 we read, "All Scripture is given by inspiration of God : . ." (literally, "is God-breathed"). It has been said that nothing is closer to a living person than his breath. The Greek word translated "inspiration" conveys the idea of a sailboat being purposefully carried by the wind to its destination. The very words of Scripture have purpose—destination—and they come from God Himself. The doctrine of inspiration is supported by Christ's own teaching on the preservation of Scripture (Matt. 5:18).

People sometimes use the terms *inspiration* and *revelation* interchangeably, but they are not really the same. "Revelation" should be used only for those parts of Scripture which the writer could not know unless God communicated them to him. For instance, Moses (the writer of Genesis) could not have known how God created the universe if God had not "revealed" it to him. On the other hand, many parts of the Bible are records of what the writer saw or did or learned from others. These writers were "inspired" by God to write certain incidents of history and to omit many others. Why this selection? The Holy Spirit has given us in the Bible just what we need, and no more. "All Scripture . . . is profitable." Thus we can say that the Bible contains many revelations from God, but the entire Scripture is inspired by Him. *Plenary inspiration* means that all parts of Scripture and all subjects dealt with in Scripture are fully inspired. *Verbal inspiration* means that the very words of Scripture are inspired. These statements will be seen to be true when we consider what the Bible says about itself.

The Old Testament Is Inspired

The Old Testament claims to be inspired. A good deal of it constitutes the very words of God Himself. Often in the Old Testament we read, "Thus says the LORD" or "God spoke to . . ." etc. These phrases and similar ones are found thousands of times in the Old Testament. All sixteen of the writing prophets from Isaiah to Malachi were God's messengers, delivering God's word to His people (and even sometimes to their enemies). What is more, Christ taught that the Old Testament—that is, the Law (Matt. 5:18; Mark 7:8), the Prophets (John 6:45), and the other Writings (Luke 16:29-31; John 17:17)—were God's word. The apostles, too, believed that the Old Testament was inspired. For instance, Peter said, "The Holy Spirit spoke by the mouth of David . . ." (Acts 1:16) and wrote, "Holy men of God spoke as they were moved by the Holy Spirit . . ." (2 Pet. 1:21). And Paul proclaimed, "The Holy Spirit spoke by Isaiah the prophet to our fathers . . ." (Acts 28:25).

The New Testament Is Inspired

When Christ was on earth He made a remarkable promise to His disciples recorded in John 14:26: He said, "The Holy Spirit . . . will bring to your remembrance all things that I said to you" (John 14:26). This "inspiration" from the Holy Spirit would help them write the Gospels. Christ also promised, "When He, the Spirit of truth, has come, He will guide you into all truth" (John 16:13). This would help them to write the Letters (Epistles), which give us the wonderful instruction for the church. Christ also said of the Holy Spirit, "He will tell you things to come" (John 16:13). This promise was fulfilled partly when John wrote the book of Revelation and partly when other apostles wrote prophetic passages. Thus we can say with confidence that the New Testament is inspired by God.

New Testament writers realized that they were controlled by the Spirit (carried along, as in the picture of the sailboat given above). Paul wrote, "God has revealed them to us by His Spirit" (1 Cor. 2:10). "The things which I write to you are the commandments of the Lord" (1 Cor. 14:37). "By revelation [God] made known to me the mystery" (Eph. 3:3, 5). "The Spirit expressly says . . ." (1 Tim. 4:1). John knew he was inspired to pen what he did (see Revelation 1:1; 14:13; 19:9).

Both Peter (1 Pet. 1:12) and Paul (Gal. 1:12) knew that the gospel was from God. These men had known from youth that the Old Testament was inspired of God. The Holy Spirit showed them that the New Testament was equally inspired. For instance, in 1 Corinthians 15:3-4 the Gospels are linked with the Old Testament Scriptures and put on the same plane with them. The death, burial, and resurrection of Christ are recorded as being "according to the Scriptures." In 1 Timothy 5:18, Paul quotes from both Deuteronomy and the gospel of Luke and calls them "the Scriptures." In 1 Peter 1:25, the gospel message is put on a level with the word of the Lord in Isaiah; both are inspired and eternal. In 2 Peter 3:2, the apostles are linked with the prophets, and in verse 16 Peter link's Paul's epistles with "the other Scriptures." Consider Proverbs 30:5-6, which amounts to a summary and a practical warning at this point:

Every word of God is pure; He is a shield to those who put their trust in Him. Do not add to His words, lest He rebuke you, and you be found a liar.

Limits to Inspiration

We have seen that the Bible teaches it is both fully and verbally inspired by God. To help us understand what this means, we will also consider what it does *not* mean.

First, the original writers retained their *individuality*. Although each was being guided by the Holy Spirit in what they penned, the personality of the writer was not destroyed. Each author expressed his own individuality in noticeable ways. For example, the style and ministry of Jeremiah are quite different from those of Isaiah or Ezekiel. Matthew, a Jew, wrote his gospel especially for the Jews, but Luke, a Gentile, seems to have had the Greeks especially in mind. It is worth noting that the personalities of Paul, Peter, James, and John shine out through their respective inspired writings.

Second is the *absence of all the original manuscripts* (termed *autographs*) of all the divinely chosen authors. They were 'lost" long ago. God, in His wisdom, allowed this to happen, no doubt to avoid their becoming objects of worship (compare 2 Kings 18:4). However, God has sovereignly ensured that very excellent copies have been preserved, and they are essentially the same as the original documents.

Third is the issue of *translations*. Due to differences between languages, it is impossible to have a perfect translation. However, the translations we have are fully reliable for study and devotional reading. Bible translations that ECS Ministries recommends are *The New King James Version* (on which this ECS courses is based), *The New American Standard Bible, The English Standard Version, The NET Bible,* and *The Authorized (King James) Version.* Some Bible versions are really more of a paraphrase than a translation. The student should keep in mind that the easy-to-read versions generally sacrifice some exactness of thought in order to make the English wording as fluent as possible.

Fourth is the evidence of *restraint*. Sometimes the authors would have liked to write more, but the Holy Spirit restrained them. For instance, in the book of Revelation, John was about to record the message of the seven thunders, but was told not to do so (10:4). The writer of Hebrews wanted to write about Melchizedek (5:11), but was prevented. Jude planned to write about salvation, but instead found it necessary to exhort the saints earnestly to contend for the faith (v. 3). Whether or not they realized it, in all they wrote or did *not* write, the Bible authors were being directed by the Spirit of God.

2

BIBLIOLOGY:
THE STUDY OF THE BIBLE
– PART 2 –

The Canon of Scripture

The word *canon* is used to describe the sixty-six books of the Bible. The term means a "reed," a "measure," or "rule," and suggests the testing of books to see if they meet the divine standard. There are many ancient religious books; how do we know that only these sixty-six books in our Bible today are inspired, and no others? After all, the Roman Catholic Church puts fourteen ancient books (called the *Apocrypha*) on the same level as the Bible, including certain additions to canonical books, like Daniel.

How the Bible Came to Be Written

It is important to take into account the history of how the Old and New Testament canons came about.

The Hebrew patriarchs (Abraham, Isaac, and Jacob) highly valued the precious promises from God concerning a land that would be theirs and a nation of people that couldn't be numbered. Important events from their lives were written down, usually on clay or stone tablets, and passed on from father to son as a valuable heritage. In writing the *Pentateuch* (the first five books in the Bible) Moses may have incorporated this written material as a revelation from God and added his own records up until the time of his death. As the people of Israel traveled through the wilderness and entered the land of Canaan, these records were zealously guarded. Other books were written by the early prophets and added to the collection. These are the *historical books*, Joshua through 2 Kings. The *Poetic Writings* and most of the *Major and Minor Prophets* were written during this era, followed by other books of the Old Testament, some of which fall into the post-exilic period. After the prophet Malachi passed off the scene, the Old Testament was complete. No inspired writer or prophetic voice was known in Israel until New Testament times, over four hundred years later.

The twenty-seven books of the New Testament were written over a much shorter period of time and collected soon thereafter. Neither John the Baptist nor Jesus Christ wrote any books. After Pentecost, when the apostles began to preach Christ, they quoted His words from memory. Later, these sayings were written down in the four books that became known as *the Gospels*. Luke added a historical record of the expansion of the church from Jerusalem to Rome (Acts). The apostles also established churches and wrote nineteen *letters* to build up the new converts. To these were added the letters of James, Jude, and the book of Revelation.

Not all these twenty-seven books were accepted unanimously from the very start, although most were. Many controversies raged, but in the year 397, at the Council of Carthage, the canon of the New Testament as we know it was finally certified. It is important to realize that the books were actually canonical as soon as they were written, since they were divinely inspired. The Council merely gave formal recognition to a widely held belief from earliest times. (If this topic interests you, read *The Formation of the New Testament* by Chuck Gianotti, published by ECS Ministries.)

> **The books were actually canonical as soon as they were written, since they were divinely inspired.**

The Tests of Canonicity

Why do Christians today accept the thirty-nine books of the Old Testament and no others? One reason is that all except Ruth, Ezra, Ecclesiastes, Song of Solomon, and a few of the Minor Prophets are quoted by the writers of the New Testament as authoritative. No important doctrine is based exclusively on any one of these books, and the Old Testament as a whole was endorsed by the Lord Jesus Himself (Luke 24:27).

Furthermore, through the era of the early church, we can accept the testimony of the Holy Spirit to the acceptability of these books and to the New Testament books, though some individuals did doubt a few books for a time. The sixty-six books of the Bible all speak of Christ and glorify Him. On the other hand, the books of the Apocrypha contain historical and geographical errors. They seem to justify falsehood, prayers for the dead, and salvation by good works—all of which are unscriptural concepts. The Apocrypha never formed a part of the Hebrew Old Testament, nor does it today.

Progress of Doctrine

Another point to consider is what is known as the *progress of doctrine*. The doctrine of inspiration does not imply that any one inspired book or passage contains all the truth on a particular subject. It does, however, assert that there is no contradiction in the various passages concerning a subject. For example, Genesis teaches much about God, but it does not teach *everything* about God. Each book of the Bible adds more teaching about the person, work, and glory of our Creator. In fact, the whole of the Bible does not attempt to tell us *everything* about God, since this would be beyond human comprehension. The Bible contains everything that God has been pleased to reveal about Himself. Nothing can be added to God's written Word, as it is perfectly suited to man as he is.

The progress of doctrine may be seen in the doctrines about Christ, the Holy Spirit, salvation, and other subjects. By and large, the Old Testament emphasizes the righteousness of God, whereas the New Testament brings God's grace prominently before us. The pinnacle of revealed truth is found in the epistles of Paul, but even these would be hard to understand without the background of the Old Testament and the other books of the New Testament. The canon of Scripture is, of course, now complete.

The progress of doctrine can also be observed in the Bible through dispensations in that each dispensation brought to man more light from God. A *dispensation* is a divinely ordained dealing with man by God in a certain time period (e.g., the dispensations of law in the Old Testament era or of grace in the New). We believe, as the Bible teaches, that the one true God revealed Himself from time to time through His servants in an ever more wonderful way.

The Interpretation of Scripture

Most of the Bible is written in simple language, so it was evidently intended to bless common people. Some passages, however, challenge the greatest minds, and even the simpler ones have untold depth. The doctrine of inspiration does not assert that there are no problems in Scripture interpretation! In some passages it is hard to know what the Holy Spirit intends us to understand. Some sections are simple, straightforward narrative, while others are better understood as being pictorial or metaphorical.

The problem of interpreting Scripture is accentuated by the teaching of certain false cults which base their teachings on the Bible. This is true to some extent of practically all the cults of Christendom. The study of the correct principles of interpretation is called *hermeneutics*. Many books have been written on hermeneutics, the better ones of which provide principles of interpretation that are biblical and helpful to all Bible students. Let us briefly examine here some of the most important principles for interpreting God's Word.

First of all, in all Bible interpretation it is important to differentiate between *observation* (what is in the text), *interpretation* (what it means), and *application* (what it means to us now, especially in practical terms). There is only one primary meaning to each passage, although spiritual implications and applications may be numerous—the Word of God is such a storehouse of truth! Interpretation is important: not only does it help us see what God is saying to us, but it helps bridge the gap between the ancient writers and our modern times. Only a born-again person who is reverently dependent on the Holy Spirit to teach him or her will consistently interpret correctly. The many conflicting interpretations of the Bible are largely due to unscriptural (but often scholarly) men forcing their own ideas upon the sacred text.

The overall rule of all interpretation is to take every statement in its ordinary, normal meaning if it makes sense. Figures of speech abound in Scripture, but these too convey literal truth. The following seven principles, while not exhaustive, will greatly aid the student's thinking.

1. We must trace truth all the way through the Bible, as the initial revelation will not be the last word on a subject, though it may be the key to the subject (progress of doctrine). It is wrong,

however, to say that early revelation is "lower" in value than later revelation. Dispensational studies greatly facilitate the understanding of progressive revelation.

2. God devised human language and then condescended to communicate through it. In so doing, He used human expressions to get His ideas across. This is primarily true of explaining His own attributes by using *anthropopathisms* (see the later lesson on God's personal attributes). God reveals through written words and is not hindered from communicating just because human language is imperfect. He has accommodated Himself to how we comprehend things.

3. Instead of forcing preconceived notions from one's own denominational or credal background on the Bible and searching for "proof-texts," the honest thing to do is to follow through all the verses on a given subject and then draw the conclusions warranted by those verses.

4. Words, grammar, expressions, etc., should all be seen in their proper context and historical framework. As the saying goes, "A text taken out of context results in pretext."

5. The same grammatical, historical interpretation should be used throughout Scripture, making allowances for obvious poetic and metaphorical expressions. Some people take the Bible literally except for prophecies—this is an unwarranted differentiation. For example, the prophecies of Christ's first advent were fulfilled literally; therefore, those of His second coming and kingdom will also be fulfilled literally. It is unscriptural to "spiritualize" (explain away by allegorizing) such things as the millennium.

6. The Bible, as a divine book, cannot teach more than one system of faith. Theologians call this rule *the analogy of faith*. It cannot, for example, teach both the eternal security of the believer and the "falling away" doctrine at the same time! There are, however, different emphases and dispensational distinctions to observe in interpreting the Bible. Cross references and parallel passages will help clarify the real teaching of God on a subject.

7. A person may gain a phenomenal knowledge of God's Word from translations, especially if he uses modern aids such as devout and scholarly commentaries, concordances, dictionaries,

and lexicons. These resources are good enough for the majority of Bible students. However, the final authority in any controversy must be the Hebrew text of the Old Testament and the Greek of the New, since these are the predominant languages God chose to use as His media of communication. A knowledge of these languages does not clear up all difficulties, though it does reveal which difficulties are merely in the translations and which are part of the original texts.

For a more in-depth study of hermeneutics, study the ECS course *Study to Show Yourself Approved*.

The Illumination of Scripture

The word *illumination* is used to describe the flooding of physical objects with light. We use the same word to describe the Holy Spirit's flooding of the inspired revelation of God with spiritual light. The principles of interpretation we have just considered will result in true understanding only if the

> The Bible is the final authority for Christian faith and practice.

Author of the Bible, the Holy Spirit, who inspired the text through human writers, illuminates the Word (1 Cor. 2:10-14; 1 John 2:20, 27). Illumination does not concern the impartation of new knowledge (revelation) or the accurate recording of that revelation (inspiration), but the clarification of the text as it stands, revealed and inspired of God. It is important to keep these differences in mind.

Some people say we cannot trust the Bible because some verses seem to contradict others. Practically all of the so-called contradictions, when studied carefully, can be resolved. They actually tend to bring out more clearly the beauties of Scripture. We may attribute the remaining "contradictions" to man's limited ability to understand the infinite wisdom and knowledge of God.

Because the Bible is *inerrant* (free from error) and *infallible* (incapable of error), it is the final authority for Christian faith and practice. The humblest believer can go to it assured that the Holy Spirit will illumine the Word to his heart and mind, answer his spiritual questions, and satisfy his deepest longings. The rest of the lessons in this series will be based strictly on this divine authority, the Word of God.

3

THEOLOGY PROPER: THE STUDY OF GOD – PART 1 –

The literal meaning of the word *theology* is "the study of God." But as the word has taken on a wider meaning, embracing the whole area of Christian doctrine, writers generally use the term *Theology Proper* for the more specific study of the person of God.

The Existence of God

Apart from the Bible we cannot know a great deal about God, although we can learn some things from natural reason. There are four chief logical arguments for the existence of God, the first three of which have biblical support.

There is **the cosmological argument**. According to this argument, the universe is an effect which must have an adequate cause. If something now exists, it must either have come from nothing or be eternal. Nothing has ever been demonstrated to be uncaused, or to come from nothing. It is more logical to believe in an eternal Supreme Intelligence creating things and creatures out of nothing than to believe that matter is eternal. It may be concluded from this argument that God is the eternal, powerful "Cause" great enough to produce such a complex and magnificent "effect" as the universe (Gen. 1:1; Heb. 11:3).

Then there is **the teleological argument**. There is, according to this reasoning, observable purpose, design, and order in the universe that must be accounted for. This is closely related to the first argument. Paul used this argument in Acts 14:17 when speaking of the orderly progression of the seasons as a sign of God's goodness to man. A popular analogy is the illustration of the man who finds a watch and, after observing its working order and complexity, reasons back to an intelligent maker. The classic presentation of this is in Paley's *Natural Theology,* an old but great book which Darwinism sought to disprove.

The question of suffering and evil in the world is often brought up against the teleological argument. However, we must remember that God did not create evil or suffering; these are negative things, the results of Satan's and man's disobedience to God. We must remember too that, in the end, God will be shown to have been just and wise in all His ways.

Next, there is **the anthropological argument**. A further refinement of the first two arguments, this line of reasoning says that the intellectual, emotional (including religious), and volitional aspects of man's nature demand an intelligent Cause with somewhat similar attributes. Quoting a heathen philosopher (who for once spoke truly), Paul told his audience in Athens (Acts 17:28-29) that man, as God's offspring, must not think of God as an unthinking idol of stone or metal. An objection to the anthropological argument is the presence of depravity in man, but since the people who attack the existence of God seldom think of themselves as depraved, the argument is rarely brought up! We should remember that the marring of the image of God in man is the result of mankind's fall in Adam.

Finally, there is **the ontological argument**. This argument is not found in Scripture and is rejected by many, though it has helped some to believe in God. (For more information, see the ECS course *Ready to Give an Answer.*) It is a deductive argument with two premises and a conclusion—(1) I have the idea of the Most Perfect Being. (2) This Being, if He exists, is greater than a most perfect being who does not exist—that is, the idea of His actual existence is included in the concept of being the Greatest Being. (3) Therefore, as the idea of existence is included in the idea of the Most Perfect Being, that Being must exist. Many people have difficulty following the logic of the last argument, but it has been used since the Middle Ages and is at least worth knowing about.

These arguments do not contain enough light to bring man to salvation, but many times they have proved to be a step in the right direction—a belief in God. So we see that even apart from the Bible, there is strong indication in favor of a Supreme Being, whom we call God.

But what of those who think otherwise? It is only fair to consider the views of those who disbelieve in the one, true, personal God.

> Even apart from the Bible, there is strong indication in favor of a Supreme Being, whom we call God.

First, there is **atheism**. "There is no God," says the atheist. However, how can he be sure that there is no God? For a man to state positively that there is no God means that he himself must know everything! Either he knows there is no God or else he should not say so. The dogmatic atheist virtually assumes all knowledge. He would have to travel to every part of the universe to be sure there is no God. For example, when the Communists first put a man into orbit, they reported him saying he did not see God in outer space. This "confirmed" the loose thinking of unbelievers about the supposed non-existence of God. But God might have been farther out in space. As someone wittily remarked, "If Comrade Spaceman had stepped out of his spaceship, he would have met God!" To be completely sure that there is no God, the atheist would have to know everything and be everywhere at once. But these are attributes of God. So the atheist denies the existence of a supernatural being by assuming divine attributes! Without the power of God, no man can prove there is no God.

> For a man to state positively that there is no God means that he himself must know everything!

Second, there is **agnosticism**. "It's not possible to know whether or not God exists," says the agnostic. This is more reasonable than outright atheism, but it is obviously based on ignorance. The agnostic may claim that no man can know that God exists, but he cannot make a universal statement, speaking for everybody, to that effect.

Some people think that evolution proves the Bible is not true, but even if evolution were true, it would have to have had a beginning. Who formed the basic elements which are supposed to have "evolved" into the complex world around us? Who started it and keeps it going? *God* created the universe, and *God* keeps it going.

Then there is **polytheism**. This belief is the opposite of atheism: it teaches there are many gods. Religions such as those of ancient Greece and Rome or Hinduism and Shintoism today have a variety of gods, but these may be traced back to an original supreme Deity who brought the others into existence. In polytheism, creatures are exalted to the rank of gods and worshipped as such.

Next comes **pantheism**. This gross delusion teaches that God is *co-extensive* with His universe. This means that the universe is self-created and that every man is part of God. "God is all; all is God," the pantheist says, thus teaching that God is indistinguishable from His creation. This doctrine in various forms is part of the teaching of certain cults and is refuted by the biblical teaching that God is greater than and separate from His creation.

Finally, there is **deism**. While not denying that God exists, deists refuse to believe that He has revealed Himself. They say that God created the universe and then withdrew to some remote corner to let things take their own course. It is hard to understand why God would create a universe and a race of human beings in His image unless He had some purpose to communicate to man.

It is interesting to note that one sentence of God's Word—the very first verse in the Bible—refutes all the above-named false teachings!

The Attributes of God

Many people spend a whole lifetime learning more about God's creation, and surely it is a fascinating study. How much more satisfying, however, to know God Himself! We have seen that some things can be known of God's existence and power from nature and reason, but God's revelation to man, the Holy Bible, tells us very much more about God's attributes than either nature or reason does. We question how finite man can know infinite God, but the Scriptures point the *way* to understanding much about God.

> The Bible tells us much more about God's attributes than either nature or reason does.

An *attribute* is a property which is intrinsic to, or absolutely necessary to, its subject. The attributes of God are so vast a theme that it is impossible to classify them perfectly. Some have divided them into attributes that only God possesses (such as eternity and infinity), calling these *incommunicable*, and those that man possesses to a certain degree (such as love and knowledge), calling these *communicable*. Others use the words *absolute* and *relative*. In this lesson the divisions will be between the attributes of God that are *personal* (which man shares to some extent) and those that are *constitutional* (not communicated to man).

The Personal Attributes of God

In the anthropological argument we noted that man has intellectual, emotional, and volitional attributes, which suggest a similar make-up in the Deity. This naturally leads to a conclusion that man is in the image of God, which is exactly what the Bible teaches (Gen. 1:26). This does not mean that God is a man-shaped being like the white-bearded old man used in medieval art to represent God the Father. In John 4:24 Jesus stated that God is a Spirit-being. Expressions which refer to "God's arm" or "God's eyes" are figures of speech, or *anthropomorphisms*—they are used to clarify what attribute of God is being conveyed by comparing it with its counterpart in man's physical makeup. For example, God's "arm" is His power. The Second Person of the Blessed Trinity did, however, take on a human body, and will always possess human characteristics (in a glorified form, however). This will be taken up in the section on Christology.

Intellect

The great intellectual attribute of God is that of **omniscience**. As all men possess some intelligence, it is not difficult to grasp what all-knowing intellect would be. This is what God's omniscience is—the knowledge of all things, whether actual or possible, past, present, or future, people, events, circumstances, places, or things. Furthermore, God exercises His omniscience without effort and equally well in all fields. A good example of God's omniscience is seen in the life of God the Son, where our Lord told what would have happened if He had

> God exercises His omniscience without effort and equally well in all fields.

done His miracles in Tyre and Sidon (knowledge of the possible—Matt. 11:21ff). This doctrine is encouraging to believers, in that we can know that God saved us even while He knew how many times we would fail Him after conversion.

Sensibility

When speaking of God, the word *sensibility* is better than the word *emotions*, since the latter term might have some misleading implications. We will briefly examine four leading attributes of sensibility, or the "higher feelings."

First John 4:8 reads, "God is **love**." But what is love? Love includes both the idea of affection and correction, and may be summed up as "That which seeks the highest good of the object loved." Goodness, mercy, and grace are closely related to love but may be thought of as *expressions* of God's love rather than as separate attributes. See also Ephesians 2:4-7 and 1 John 3:1. For us to love God means we will seek His will, which is the highest good.

> For us to love God means we will seek His will, which is the highest good.

God is **just**. Liberal thinking tends to magnify the attribute of love to the point of forgetting the balancing doctrine of justice, or righteousness (those two terms translate the same word in the original texts). In redemption, God is both "just and the justifier" of the believer in Jesus (Rom. 3:26). In judgment, He "shows no partiality," meaning He judges with moral equity (Acts 10:34). Other major verses on God's righteousness, or justice, are Psalms 11:7; 145:17; John 17:25; and Revelation 16:5-7.

> We should be continually observing new areas in which we need to conform to the holiness of God.

God is **holy**. In the negative sense, holiness is the absence of evil. In the positive sense, it is the quality of active righteousness in perfection by which He eternally wills and maintains His own moral excellence. Christians have an absolute standard in God and are commanded by Him to be holy because *He* is holy (1 Peter 1:16). Though the standard is absolute, the requirements are relative to our Christian maturity. We should be continually observing new areas in which we need to conform to the holiness of God. In this day of unholy living, the dazzling holiness of God must be emphasized to bring out in sharp contrast the exceeding sinfulness of sin. Read also Isaiah 6:3, John 17:11, and Revelation 4:8.

God is **truth**. Our Lord Jesus Christ said that He is the way, the truth, and the life (John 14:6). Truth is one of the leading properties of Deity. Like holiness, it has both a negative and a positive side. Truth is both the absence of falsehood and the positive agreement to what is represented—that is, consistency to a standard. Since God Himself is the standard, this is the same as saying that God is self-consistent. Paul states in Romans 3:4, "Let God be true but every man a liar." Because of this attribute of truth, we may be assured that the Lord God can do nothing false in His purposes, His promises, or His revelation. That His revelation of Himself is true is an argument for the inerrancy of His holy Word, a doctrine that has received attacks even from supposed defenders of the evangelical cause.

Will

Independence from restraint or restriction is called *freedom,* so we can rightly state that God is completely **free**. With respect to man, freedom is a relative term, since no creature is free to do exactly as he pleases. With respect to God, freedom means the

———— ✍ ————

God has all power to carry out His perfect will.

———— ✍ ————

unrestricted independence to do as He sees fit. Of course, God will not act contrary to His nature, but since His nature is perfection, this can hardly be considered a restriction. He may impose "restraints" on Himself in the form of promises or covenants, and He will act within these programs, but only because He has decided to do so. God is not obligated to do anything for sinful man, but where He has committed Himself—such as in His promises to Abraham, and the offer of free salvation to all who receive His Son—He will carry out His word. A beautiful passage on the freedom of God is found in Isaiah 40:6-31.

God is **omnipotent**. Not only does God have freedom to will what He desires, but He has all power—omnipotence—to carry out His perfect will. Many times in Scripture, God is called "Almighty" (same meaning as "omnipotent"). Job said to God, "I know that You can do everything" (Job 42:2). God's great power is seen in the creation and preservation of the universe, the exodus from Egypt, the resurrection of Christ, and the salvation of lost sinners. It has been said that creation was just "finger-play" to God (Psalm 8), but it took the arm of the Lord to save lost mankind (Isa. 53:1). What is meant by this is

————— ❧ —————

Creation was just "finger-play" to God (Psalm 8), but it took the arm of the Lord to save lost mankind (Isa. 53:1).

————— ❧ —————

that whereas creation was accomplished through the spoken word of God, it took the death of His Son to provide redemption for fallen humanity. See also Jeremiah 32:17; Matthew 19:26, and Revelation 19:6.

In the next chapter, we will study the constitutional attributes of God.

4

THEOLOGY PROPER: THE STUDY OF GOD – PART 2 –

The constitutional attributes of God are much harder to comprehend than His personal attributes, since by their very nature they cannot be communicated to man to possess.

The Constitutional Attributes of God

First there is His **simplicity.** God is uncompounded—that is, He is a pure Spirit-being (John 4:24). This attribute relates to His essence.

Then there is His **unity.** "Hear, O Israel, The LORD our God, the LORD is one!" (Deut. 6:4). For centuries the Jews have proclaimed the unity of God with these words. God is one in being, essence, and power. The word for *one* in the *Shema* ("Hear," as this little creed is called) does not refer to stark numerical oneness; rather, it suggests the union of persons hinted at in the Hebrew plural name of God, *Elohim*. It is important to make clear that Christians, like the faithful ones in the Old Testament, believe in only *one* God, not three, as is sometimes falsely charged.

> God is one in being, essence, and power.

Next there is His **infinity.** God is unbounded, limitless, and unconfined to temples made with hands (1 Kings 8:27). God transcends space altogether; it too was created by Him.

Then there is His **eternality**. Eternity is the time-relationship of infinity; God transcends time altogether as well. In time we are bounded by the temporal succession of events. In eternity there will be no such succession, though there will probably be progression. A feeble illustration of God's relationship to time is the sight that a person on top of a high building gets of an entire parade, from start to finish, compared with the momentary view that those on the streets get of just one part of the parade at a time when it is passing before his eyes. "From everlasting to everlasting, You are God" (Ps. 90:2).

There is His **immutability**. God is unchanging and unchangeable. There can be no development or contradiction in His personality (James 1:17). Passages such as Genesis 6:6, where God is said to "repent" (that is, to change His mind), merely speak to accommodating to man's viewpoint of things by ascribing human emotions or will to a deity. This is called an *anthropopathism*. In the outworking of His purpose, the revelation of God's plan in sequence gives the impression to man that He has changed His mind. God will never change His attributes. When a man obeys God, God will act one way, and when he disobeys, He will act in another according with His divine nature, but there is no change in God Himself.

> **Christians should practice living in the presence of the Lord as a spiritual reality.**

In addition, there is His **omnipresence**. This attribute has been called the infinity of God in relation to His creation and creatures. God is every*where,* but He is not every*thing,* as pantheism teaches. It is possible to be indwelt by the Spirit of God but to be out of fellowship with Him, and hence "far from the Lord" in a spiritual or moral sense. We cannot escape from the presence of God. Christians should practice living in the presence of the Lord as a spiritual reality. Psalm 139:7-10 is the classic passage that depicts God's omnipresence.

> **The sovereignty of God is a reassuring doctrine to the faithful, especially when things seem to go against right and truth.**

Finally, there is His **sovereignty**. To say that God is sovereign is to say that He is the Supreme Ruler; it says nothing about what *kind* of sovereignty He exercises. He is the Ultimate Ruler and is never "caught off guard." The sovereignty of God is a reassuring doctrine to the faithful, especially when things seem to go against right and truth. In the final analysis, everything will work out for the glory of God, including things that are evil in themselves and are opposed to His plan. God's sovereignty is presented in Romans 9:14-24 and Ephesians 1:3-14. The Bible also teaches that man is a responsible moral agent. It is impossible to reconcile this in our minds with God's sovereignty—nevertheless, both teachings are divinely revealed as true. It is dangerous to over-emphasize one at the expense of the other.

The Trinity

If scientists and psychologists have a hard time defining human personality, it should not surprise us that theologians and other students of Bible doctrine find it difficult to describe God. One of the most difficult mysteries of God's being is the doctrine of the Trinity. The word itself does not occur in the Bible, but the truth of it permeates the

> The word "Trinity" does not occur in the Bible, but the truth of it permeates the book.

book. Let us look at a couple of definitions of the Trinity and then see how they were arrived at from the Scriptures themselves.

One well-known definition is contained in the Westminster Confession of Faith (1643): "In the Unity of the Godhead there be three Persons of one substance, power, and eternity . . ."

This is quite a scriptural statement of the doctrine of the Trinity. However, the word "Persons" could be misleading, since it does not mean persons in the ordinary sense of individual people. There are not three Gods. God is three in a different sense than He is one, so there is really no contradiction. This truth is emphasized in B. B. Warfield's definition: "In the unity of the Godhead there are three co-eternal and co-equal Persons: the same in substance, but distinct in subsistence." The word "unity" here safeguards the usual but rather difficult term "persons," and the words "co-equal" and "co-eternal" avoid the implication that the Son and the Spirit are inferior to, or created by, the Father. The three persons of the "Tri-unity," as someone has more clearly termed the Godhead, are of one substance or essence. In science it is well known that each element reveals a characteristic and unique pattern on the spectroscope, and an element always has the same pattern. Likewise, each person in the Godhead has the same "pattern," since the Persons are one in essence.

The doctrine of the Trinity is not spelled out in the Bible, but it is the only logical solution to seeming contradictions therein. As we have seen, the Bible clearly teaches that God is one (Deut. 6:4). At the same time, it teaches that the Father is God, the Son is God, and the Holy Spirit is God. No one argues against the deity of the Father, but it is necessary to convince some of the deity of the Son and of the Spirit.

God the Son

Christ is distinct from the Father, but He is God also. Consider, for example, John 1:1: "The Word was with God, and the Word was God." Here we see Christ (literally) "face to face with" God—hence, distinct from Him—yet also called God. Christ is called God in Hebrews 1:8 and John 20:28.

Christ is also God because He possesses the attributes of God—for example, His immutability (Heb. 13:8); His omnipresence (Matt. 18:20), and His omniscience (John 2:24-25).

A third proof that Christ is God is His divine works. In Mark 2:5-7, Christ forgives sin, clearly a prerogative of Deity alone. In Colossians 1:16-17, Christ is seen not only as Creator of the universe, but also as its Sustainer. More attention to Christ's deity will be given in chapter 5, Christology – Part 1.

God the Holy Spirit

By the same three proofs, the Holy Spirit is God. He is clearly called God in Acts 5, as a comparison of verses 3 and 4 will show. See also 1 Corinthians 3:16.

The Spirit likewise has the attributes of the Father and Son, such as eternality (Heb. 9:14), omniscience (1 Cor. 2:10-11), and omnipresence. He indwells every Christian (1 Cor. 6:19).

Divine works of the Spirit include regeneration (John 3:5; Titus 3:5), conviction of sin (John 16:7-11), and inspiration of the written Word of God (2 Pet. 1:21).

If there were three Gods, they would all have divine characteristics, so when arguing the case for the doctrine of the Trinity it is not enough to show the deity of each person of the Godhead—the unity of these Three must be demonstrated also. Matthew 28:19 associates the persons of the Trinity under one name (notice the single word "name" with the three persons mentioned). The apostolic benediction in 2 Corinthians 13:14 also puts the three together on one level, as do the accounts of our Lord's baptism (Matt. 3:16-17).

All of the proofs for the Trinity listed so far have been taken from the New Testament. This is logical. During Old Testament times, the dangers of polytheism were so great that the unity of God had to be stressed (Deut. 6:4); once Israel was "cured" of idolatry by the Babylonian captivity, however, the teaching of the triune nature of God could be more clearly revealed. The Trinity is contained in the Old Testament, but not explicitly. The very Hebrew word for "God," *Elohim* (the "-im" ending being the same as in "cherubim" and "seraphim"), is in the plural form even though it is used with a singular verb. This observation ties in with the clearer New Testament revelation. In Psalm 2 the Messiah and God the Father are differentiated but both clearly divine, as are the Spirit and the Father in Isaiah 48:16.

> **During Old Testament times, the dangers of polytheism were so great that the unity of God had to be stressed.**

The problem of understanding the Trinity remains, but this should not surprise us. If we cannot understand everything about God's creation even with the help of ongoing scientific discoveries, why should we be surprised if we cannot analyze God's own nature or personality? To be surprised at not being able to comprehend the deity or Trinity is to be surprised at not being God.

It is better to simply believe God's revelation and understand as much as He has graciously deigned to reveal to us. For the present, we can confidently say the Bible teaches throughout that there is only one God, that He has existed eternally as Father, Son, and Holy Spirit, and that these Three are equally God. The believer in Jesus Christ has no real difficulty accepting the beautiful teaching of the Trinity, as it alone accounts for the eternal exercise of the love of God between the persons of the Godhead, and long before anything was created. With saints and angels, we may well join in praising the one true God in His threefold personality.

God the Father

One of the most meaningful concepts in regard to God is that the first person of the Trinity is called "Father." The human idea of fatherhood in the best sense is derived from the divine. Holy Scripture presents God as Father in four important and distinct senses.

He is **the Father of all creation**. Due to the unscriptural emphasis of liberals on the so-called "universal fatherhood of God and brotherhood of man," the scriptural truth that God is Father (Originator) of all things has been obscured among evangelicals. Acts 17:28-29 presents God as the Supplier of life and material needs for mankind. And in a limited way, all human beings *are* "brothers," being of common descent from Adam, who is called a son of God (Luke 3:38). In the spirit sense, however, there is a huge gulf between the saved and the lost.

He is **the Father of Israel**. As a nation, Israel had God as its Father, for He called Israel His "son" and His "firstborn" (Ex. 4:22). In Jeremiah 31:9, He said explicitly, "I am a Father to Israel." It is important to note that this relationship is not the personal, individual relationship that now exists between the Christian believer and God and which has been made possible through Christ's atoning death. It is a national fatherhood.

He is **the Father of our Lord Jesus Christ**. The Lord Jesus often spoke of God as His Father, and prayed to Him as such. This usage occurs twenty times in Matthew, twice in Mark, eleven times in Luke, sixty-two times in John, and three times in Revelation. Paul wrote of "the God and Father of our Lord Jesus Christ" in six separate passages. Peter used the same expression in his first epistle, and John used similar language four times. It is not to be imagined that this Father-Son relationship is merely on the same level as that of ordinary men, or Israel, or even born-again believers. In a very special way, God acknowledged Christ as His Son: on two occasions He spoke from heaven and said, "This is My beloved Son, in whom I am well pleased."

The fact that Jesus Christ is God's Son does not mean that the Son was created or came into being by an act of God. Under Christology we shall study verses which prove that the Son is eternal. But there are two words used in Scripture which describe the relationship between the Father and the Son. First, He is the *only-begotten*. This term is used five times of Christ in John's gospel and his first epistle. The Greek word means "one of a kind," "only," or "unique." He is also the *firstborn*. This word is used seven times of Christ. When used concerning His birth of the Virgin Mary, the word means first in time (that is, the first child born to her; she would go on to bear others). In all other instances, the word means first in position (Col. 1:15). Note also the phrases "the firstborn from the dead" (Col. 1:18), and "the firstborn among many brethren" (Rom. 8:29). In any relationship with created beings, Christ must have the preeminent place.

> *Word*
>
> The fact that Jesus Christ is God's Son does not mean that the Son was created.

In the Old Testament, the word "firstborn" is often given to men who were not born first chronologically in their families. For instance, the blessings of the firstborn were given to Shem, Isaac, Jacob, Judah, and Solomon. Likewise, when used of Christ, the word "firstborn" refers to His position, not to His origin. As man, of course, He was not first in the world. As the Son of God, He was never brought into being or begotten in the sense that a human son is engendered by a male forebear. Many people believe that the use of the terms "Father" and "Son" when speaking of God is largely anthropomorphic anyway—in other words, the nearest human equivalent is being used to describe a divine fact. At any rate, the Father-Son relationship has always existed between God the Father and God the Son, and this is called *eternal generation* or *eternal sonship*.

He is **the Father of Christian believers**. God is the Father of all Christians, "the children of God" (Gal. 3:26). Contrary to popular thought, not all people in the world are children of God in the spiritual sense, although, as was noted earlier in this chapter, all human beings are offspring of the Father in a creatorial sense.

It is very instructive to note that just as in ordinary life there are three ways to get into a family—by birth, adoption, and marriage—each of these parallels an act of God in or for a believer or the church as a whole. First, we get into a family by *birth*—this is the most common way. In a spiritual way, we receive authority to become children of God by receiving Christ, by believing on His name (John 1:12-13). This is known as regeneration (Titus 3:5). Second, we can gain entrance into a family by *adoption*. The word "adoption" is used in the New Testament, but as we shall see later, in a different sense from our common idea. Third, we can get into a family by *marriage*. In the New Testament, the church is described as the bride of Christ (Eph. 5:25).

——————— ✿ ———————

What a blessing it is to be in God's family and to know God as our heavenly Father!

——————— ✿ ———————

The new birth is particularly the work of the Holy Spirit (John 3:5); adoption is connected with the Father (Gal. 4:5-6); and the Son is waiting for His bride (Rev. 19:7). What a blessing it is to be in God's family and to know God as our heavenly Father!

5

CHRISTOLOGY:
THE STUDY OF CHRIST
– PART 1 –

The term *Christology* literally means "the study of Christ," which includes all that Jesus Christ has done, is doing, and will do in the future. Christ is the supreme revelation of all that is in the heart of the Father. Christ is our Savior, High Priest, and Example, the source of every blessing to us. His cross is

> —— ✦ ——
>
> **Christ is the supreme revelation of all that is in the heart of the Father.**
>
> —— ✦ ——

the center of two eternities. Everything before Christ pointed forward to Him, and all present and future blessings flow from Him and look back to His finished work on Calvary.

The Pre-incarnate Work of Christ

We have seen that Christ, as the second person of the Godhead, has always existed. What does the Scripture tell us about His work before He was born into this world? Well, it speaks of His work of **creation** and **preservation**. One evidence of the deity of Christ is His power in creating the universe. "In Him was life" (John 1:4), and He communicated that life to the world. Through the Son, God created the worlds, or ages (Heb. 1:2; John 1:3). In the New Testament we see that the Son sustains the universe by His mighty word (Heb. 1:3), and that "in Him [Christ] all things consist" (Col. 1:17, lit. "hold together").

The Scripture also tells of the work of the Son in **revelation**. Even before He became a man, the eternal Son of God revealed God to human beings. In Old Testament times, He appeared in the form of a man, sometimes as the angel of the Lord (see lesson on Angelology), and sometimes as a flame of fire. God appeared to Abraham (Gen. 12:7), Isaac (Gen. 26:2), Jacob (Gen. 35:9), Moses (Ex. 3:2), Israel (Lev. 9:4), Joshua (Josh. 5:13-15), Gideon (Judges 6:12), Manoah (Judg. 13:11), Samuel (1 Sam. 3:21), David (2 Chron. 3:1), Solomon (1 Kings 9:2), Isaiah (Isa. 6:1), Ezekiel (Ezek. 1:28), and Daniel (Dan. 10:5). There is no evidence that either the Father or the Holy Spirit revealed themselves to human beings as the Son has.

The wonderful thing is that God has revealed Himself to man through the Son.

The Deity of Christ

By His names, by being called God in so many words (e.g., Heb. 1:8), but most especially by His attributes, Jesus Christ is seen to be the divine Son of God. Under Trinitarianism we have seen some of this evidence brought forth to prove Christ's equality (and hence His deity) with the Father and the Spirit. Now we must see how Christ is both God and man in one person. He is the *Theanthropic Person,* or the "God-man."

> Jesus Christ is equally God and man, possessing at the same time perfect humanity and perfect deity, not a part of each.

It is important to realize that Jesus Christ is not a God who turned into a man; nor was He a man so good that He became a God. He is equally God and man, possessing at the same time perfect humanity and perfect deity, not a part of each. Most heresies regarding the person of our Lord veer too much in either direction on this point. Early heresies claimed that Jesus was a God who only appeared to be a man—a phantom. Today the heresies tend to say He was not truly God. A fine summary of the true position of Scripture is found in Article II of the "Articles of Religion" of the Church of England:

> The Son, which is the Word of the Father, begotten from everlasting of the Father, the very and eternal God, and of one substance with the Father, took Man's nature in the womb of the blessed Virgin, of

her substance: so that two whole and perfect Natures, that is to say, the Godhead and Manhood, were joined together in one Person, never to be divided, whereof is one Christ, very God, and very Man.

Since the deity of Christ is so much under attack, we will underscore here the truth of this doctrine by examining more fully some of His divine attributes.

His eternality. John 1:1 states that the Word—a few verses later identified as Christ—existed in the beginning. He did not come into existence in the beginning. However far back we may put the "beginning," the Word *was* at that time. In John 1:14 we see that the "Word" was Christ. He shared the Father's glory before the universe was created (John 17:5). Compare also Philippians 2:6, Colossians 1:17; 2:9, and Hebrews 1:8.

> Many people accept the worship of other people, but Jesus Christ is the only person who actually deserves it.

His preeminence (Col. 1:18). The Son is equal to God in all respects. He claimed equality with God: "I and My Father are one" (John 10:30). Christ accepted worship as God; read Matthew 14:33; John 9:38; and Luke 24:52 for three instances of this. Many people accept the worship of other people, but Jesus Christ is the only person who actually deserves it. One day, every knee will bow before Him (Phil. 2:10).

His omnipotence. In Genesis 1:1 and in many other Old Testament passages we see that God created the heavens and the earth. The New Testament records that God the Son was the One through whom all things were created (John 1:3; Col. 1:16; Heb. 1:10). When He was here in the world, the Son demonstrated divine power over nature (Mark 4:39), demons (Mark 5:8), death (Mark 5:41), disease (Luke 8:43-48), and disability (John 9).

His omniscience (John 16:30; 21:17). Many instances are recorded of Jesus knowing, revealing, and acting in response to the *thoughts* of men, including those of the Pharisees present at the healing of a paralyzed man in Matthew 9, Nathanael in John 1:48, and Simon the Pharisee in Luke 7. Christ knew (and verbalized) the details of His coming suffering, and predicted things that would happen in both the immediate future (John 6:64; 13:38) and the far future (Matthew chapters 24 & 25).

His omnipresence. Although Jesus Christ is in His resurrected human body now at the right hand of God (Eph. 1:20), He is also present with His obedient followers who are going into all the world as He commanded (Matt. 28:19-20).

His immutability (Heb. 1:12). Just as God the Father is eternally self-consistent, so is the Son of God. "Jesus Christ is the same yesterday, today, and forever" (Heb. 13:8). The greatest event of all ages was when God the Son became a man, the God-man. Even then He did not, could not, cease to be God. Nor was it possible for His wondrous character to change.

His righteousness (2 Tim. 4:8). This essential attribute of God is equally seen in the Son. He loves righteousness and hates iniquity (Heb. 1:9). In His life on earth, Christ loved sinners but hated their sins as rebellion against God. As the One into whose hands all judgment has been committed (John 5:22), the Son will judge righteously.

His holiness (Luke 1:35). One of the ways the angel Gabriel described the child that would be born to Mary was "that Holy One . . . the Son of God." We now have in heaven a holy High Priest (Heb. 7:26). The apostle Peter, a friend, recognized Christ as the Holy One (Acts 3:14), as did the demon in the demon-possessed man (Mark 1:24).

His love (John 13:1). When Christ was on earth, He was moved with compassion for people in need (e.g. Matt. 9:36). The apostle Paul described Him as loving the church and giving Himself for it (Eph. 5:25). Paul testified of Christ loving him personally, and of giving Himself for him (Gal. 2:20). It was Christ's love for Paul that prompted Paul to live for Christ.

> *Everything that God is, Christ is.*

From these verses we see that everything that God is, Christ is. It is not sufficient to say Christ is divine, if we mean by this that He is merely God-like. It will not do to say that Christ is the Son of God in the same way that all believers are sons of God. Anyone willing to face the Scripture verses in this lesson (and many more) must realize that the Bible teaches Jesus Christ is not only the Son of God (or a son of God), but God the Son.

Comparing Old and New Testament records, we observe texts like Isaiah 40:3, which predicts a forerunner coming before the Lord Jehovah comes, and that Christ is identified as the Lord in Matthew 3:1-3. The Israelites put "the LORD" to the test in their wilderness wanderings (Num. 21:6-7); this same One is stated to be Christ in 1 Corinthians 10:9. Thus we see that the Son of God is co-equal and co-eternal with the Father, "very God of very God" (from the Nicene Creed).

The Humanity of Christ

The Lord Jesus had all the characteristics of man—except a sinful nature.

His birth (apart from His miraculous conception) was normal. The Scriptures carefully state that Jesus' conception was by the Holy Spirit (Matt. 1:20), and that His mother was a virgin (1:23). Consider carefully Luke 1:31, 35; 2:5-7, 16, 21, and 28. His youth was normal. He asked questions, obeyed His parents, and "increased in wisdom and stature, and in favor with God and man" (Luke 2:40-52). He was voluntarily subject to human limitations: He experienced hunger (Matt. 4:2), tiredness (John 4:6), thirst (John 19:28). He never met His human needs by using His power as Son of God. His emotions were human, like love (Mark 10:21), anger (Mark 3:5), and sorrow (Luke 13:34). However, Jesus never showed any fear. Even when in great danger, He trusted God and was not afraid (Luke 4:29-30; John 10:31-32).

> **Jesus never showed any fear. Even when in great danger, He trusted God and was not afraid.**

His death was like a man's death, but with a difference. He did not die of exhaustion. He cried with a loud voice, and then voluntarily gave up His spirit. In John 10:17-18 He said, "I lay down My life that I may take it again. No one takes it from Me, but I lay it down of Myself." Human death is the separation of body and spirit, and Jesus did die. His nature was a man's three-fold nature; we read of His soul (Matt. 26:38), his spirit (Luke 23:46), and His body (John 19:40).

> **Jesus Christ was like all human beings in every important point—except sin.**

He was *the Perfect Man*. Jesus Christ was like all human beings in every important point—except sin. This is a very significant difference. Sin is rebellion, doing our will contrary to God's will (Rom. 1:28-32; 3:23; 5:12). God cannot act inconsistently with His own character, and neither can Christ. The Son of God cannot act contrary to the will of

God. Only Christ could truthfully say: "As My Father taught Me, I speak these things. . . . I always do those things that please Him" (John 8:28-29). Even His enemies had to admit His innocence: "Which of you convicts Me of sin?" (John 8:46). Pilate said, "I find no fault in Him" (John 19:4, 6). God the Father showed His approval of Christ: "This is My beloved Son, in whom I am well pleased" (Matt. 3:17; 17:5). Finally, God raised Him from the dead (Rom. 1:4). This above all proves that God assessed His Son a perfect man. He *did* no sin (1 Peter 2:22). He *knew* no sin (2 Cor. 5:21). In Him *was* no sin (1 John 3:5).

We have seen that Christ was a man, a perfect man. This truth is emphasized because only a man could fully reveal God to men. Only a man could die. We needed the God-man to intercede for us with God (1 Tim. 2:5). Only a sinless man could die for others. If there had been one sin in Jesus, He would have had to die for His own sin. But, praise God, the Lamb of God was perfect. The Son of God was a complete man, a sinless man. Not only did Christ not sin, but as deity in human flesh, He could not sin. He was impeccable.

> **Not only did Christ not sin, but as deity in human flesh, He could not sin.**

6

CHRISTOLOGY: THE STUDY OF CHRIST – PART 2 –

The Incarnation of Christ

We have seen that Christ has two natures, the divine and the human. The divine nature was His from eternity past, but the human nature was acquired from being born of a human woman. This taking on of flesh and blood and all it entails is called the *incarnation*, which simply means "in-flesh-ment." In order to save sinful people and be their Substitute, the eternal Son of God became a man in humble condescension. The apostle John beautifully expresses the grandeur of this doctrine of the faith in the prologue to his gospel: "And the Word became flesh and dwelt among us, and we beheld His glory, the glory as of the only begotten of the Father, full of grace and truth" (John 1:14).

That God would become man is an overpowering truth, and yet one that is suggested even in the Old Testament, where the Coming One is seen as both God and man. God gave many promises that one day a Deliverer would come. When Adam and Eve fell into sin, God had to judge them, but He also promised that the "Seed of the woman"—itself at least a hint of Christ's incarnation—would crush the enemy (Gen. 3:15). The Deliverer would be a man born to a human mother. God gave a special promise to Abraham in Genesis 22:18. The Deliverer who would bring blessing to all people would be one of Abraham's descendants. This promise was passed on to Isaac (Gen. 26:4) and to Jacob (Gen. 28:14). God promised Judah that the King would be born of his tribe (Gen. 49:10). Other promises told that the Coming One would be a Prophet like Moses (Deut. 18:15), a Priest like Melchizedek (Ps. 110:4), and a King in the line of David (2 Sam. 7:16). From these verses and many others, we learn that the coming Deliverer would not be an angel or some other being; He would be a man.

On the other hand, many promises state plainly that God Himself would come to earth. "And it will be said in that day, 'Behold, this is our God; we have waited for Him, and He will save us: this is the LORD; we have waited for Him, we will be glad and rejoice in His salvation'" (Isa. 25: 9). "Behold, the Lord GOD will come" (Isa. 40:10). John the Baptist was to "prepare the way of the LORD, make straight in the desert a highway for our God" (compare Isaiah 40:3 and John 1:23). Malachi prophesied: "The Lord, whom you seek, will suddenly come to His temple" (Mal. 3:1). Isaiah tells us some of the names of the coming King: "Wonderful, Counselor, Mighty God, Everlasting Father, Prince of Peace" (Isa. 9:6-7). Another name of Messiah is *Immanuel*, which means "God with us." He was to be born of a virgin (compare Isaiah 7:14 and Matthew 1:23).

How could the promised King and Savior be both God and man? The New Testament answer is: *only if God became a man*. This, then, is the incarnation. In Matthew 1 and Luke 2 we read the historical record of the virgin birth of Christ. In the epistles of Paul, we have the clearest possible statements of

> God had to assume a physical body to be able to die as a sacrifice for our sins.

His deity: ". . . Christ came, who is over all, the eternally blessed God" (Rom. 9:5). "The second Man is the Lord from heaven" (1 Cor. 15:47). "God was manifest in the flesh" (1 Tim. 3:16). We should also read and carefully consider these verses: Galatians 4:4; Philippians 2:6-8 and Hebrews 2:14. God had to assume a physical body to be able to die as a sacrifice for our sins.

The omnipotent Son of God could become man if He wanted to. His love tells us that He would want to, and His omnipotence shows us that He was able to. It is impossible and incredible that He should cease to be God when He became man.

Some Bible scholars assert that the Son of God give up some of His attributes when He became man. This is called the *kenosis* ("emptying") *theory*, and is based on Philippians 2:7, which says that Christ "emptied Himself" (NASB). It is biblical to say that Christ did not use His own divine powers to serve His human needs when on earth—or even to perform His miracles—but it is quite wrong to say that He did not *have* these powers. He laid aside the outward manifestation of His glory and the *independent use* of His attributes, and He did not insist upon the homage which was His by right. The attributes of God are facets of His essential being, not powers or capacities to be dispensed with at will.

The Life of Christ

Only the briefest account of the highlights of what has been termed "the greatest Life ever lived" can be included here. And in fact, even the Gospels themselves give only a selection of events and discourses of Jesus of Nazareth rather than a full biography (see the final verse in John's gospel).

There is *His nativity and childhood* (Matt. 1:18-25; Luke 2:1-10, 41-52). How divinely appropriate that God should become man by way of the miracle of the virgin birth! By an act of the Holy Spirit in the womb of the Virgin Mary, Jesus was conceived and then brought into this world as a complete human being, though without the inherited taint of original sin common to all mankind. Jesus lived about thirty-three years on this earth. From infancy to the age of about thirty there is only one incident recorded, depicting Him as the obedient and perfect boy that He was, interested in the things of His heavenly Father (Luke 2:41-52). Most of the biblical record is concerned with the three years or so of His public ministry, and especially with the week of His crucifixion (often called *Passion Week*), to which more space is given than any other comparable period recorded in the Gospels.

There is *His baptism* (Matt. 3:13-17; Mark 1:9-11; Luke 3:21-22). As Messiah, Jesus was the "Anointed One." In the Old Testament, prophets (1 Kings 19:16), priests (Ex. 28:41), and kings (2 Sam. 2:4) were all set aside for their special ministry by being anointed with oil.

At about the age of thirty, Jesus was baptized by His cousin, John the Baptist, in the River Jordan. Jesus had no sins to confess and nothing to repent of, but He accepted baptism to identify with His people (Matt. 3:15). In order that no one would think Jesus was confessing sins, God at once called Him "My beloved Son." Furthermore, the Holy Spirit came upon Him. The Spirit was given to Christ without measure (John 3:34). The anointing oil in the Old Testament is a picture or type of the Holy Spirit. At His baptism, when the Holy Spirit came upon Him in this special way, Jesus was anointed as the Christ.

There is *His temptation* (Matt. 4:1-11; Luke 4:1-13). God's public approval of Jesus as a man by calling Him His beloved Son was immediately challenged by Satan (the devil). Satan tried to prove that Jesus could not retain His position as a man without sinning, like all other human beings. God knew that Jesus, the Son of God, would never sin against Him, but Satan used all his craftiness to spoil God's plans if he could. Satan failed and Jesus won. Jesus did not sin.

There are thus two reasons for the temptation: (1) The accuser demanded his opportunity, just as he had done in the case of Job (Job 1:9-11). He might have said, "All men sin. Jesus, too, will sin." (2) God acceded in order to demonstrate to the universe the perfections of Christ. It was the Spirit who directed Jesus into the wilderness to be tempted of the devil (Matt. 4:1).

Some people argue: "Christ had to be capable of sinning, or else the temptation was meaningless." There was nothing in Christ to respond to Satan's temptation; hence it is wrong to deny His impeccability (that is, to say He could have sinned but did not). He proved His sinlessness under great stress. Some say that although as the Son of God He could not sin, as a man He could have. But this would mean that Christ had two wills, one human and one divine, which might have acted contrary to each other. This implies that Christ had a dual personality—that the Son of God merely "came upon" a man. This is a terrible heresy. If Christ could have sinned when on earth, how do we know that He cannot fail at present or in the future?

It is reassuring to know that we have an infallible Savior (Heb. 13:8) rather than just another example of a fallible man overcoming temptation. There are many examples of the latter in Scripture. The Bible teaches the perfections of Christ in every area, whereas human reasoning may lead to a Christ-dishonoring conclusion.

There are *His miracles*. The Lord Jesus performed many miracles in the power of the Holy Spirit. These were in the inanimate realm (e.g., stilling the storm); the animate realm (e.g., the miraculous catch of fish); the human realm (e.g., curing disease and raising the dead); and the spiritual realm (e.g., casting out demons).

Some have attempted to make the gospel story more palatable to unbelievers by saying that Christ had a magnetic personality and that His very presence persuaded people they were feeling better! It is hard to see how this reasoning would apply to raising the dead or stilling the storm! As so often happens, the so-called "demythologizing" explanations of Scripture which try to do away with the miraculous element are harder to believe than the matter-of-fact Bible records. Christ performed miracles because He loved the people and wanted to help them. He also proved by miracles that God was with Him (Acts 10:38). It's true that because of His miracles, many people *were* attracted to Him, but when they came, He taught them about God. Miracles also left the hard-of-heart with no excuse (John 15:24) for not believing who He said He was.

Then there is *His teaching.* Jesus did not personally write any books, but His teaching is preserved for us in the four gospel accounts. A large part of Matthew and much of Luke and John are taken up with the words of our Lord. What did Jesus teach about? He taught the people about God His Father, about the kingdom of heaven (the kingdom under God's rule), and about His own death, resurrection, and return. He often taught deeper truths by means of parables. He gave special instruction to His own disciples about the future and what it means to be His followers.

The Death of Christ

The meaning of the death of Christ and its deeper implications are found in the epistles of Paul and will be studied under Soteriology. Here we will consider only the historical aspects of Christ's death.

> When Jesus comes again, He *will* reign in glory, but first it was necessary for Him to suffer.

Since Jesus Christ did good to all men, why did the Jewish leaders reject Him? For one thing, they were expecting a king who would come in glory and deliver them from the power of Rome. Jesus came in humility and served others (Mark 10:45). When He comes again, He *will* reign in glory, but first it was necessary for Him to suffer. Jesus denounced the sin and unbelief of the people, especially the hypocrisy of the religious leaders. The scribes and Pharisees were able to turn the rabble against Christ and to demand His death.

The first "trial" was before the Sanhedrin of Jewish elders. This body condemned Him because He had claimed He was Christ, the Son of God. However, they had no authority to put anyone to death, so they delivered Him to the Roman Governor, Pontius Pilate. Pilate soon realized that Jesus had done nothing worthy of death, but in order to appease the people and avoid the possibility of losing his job, he agreed to their wishes and condemned Jesus to death by crucifixion. Jesus' friends ran away, the Jews mocked Him, and the soldiers tortured Him, but the depth of His sorrow was reached on the cross, when He cried, "My God, My God, why have You forsaken Me?" After He proclaimed "It is finished!" He expelled His own spirit. Man's guilt is fully shown in crucifying the Lord Jesus, but ultimately no man took His life from Him (John 10:17-18; Acts 2:23). Why did God forsake Him? The answer in brief is: "He [God] made Him [Christ] who knew no sin to be sin for us" (2 Cor. 5:21). The proof that God accepted Christ's atoning death is seen in that He raised Him from the dead (Rom. 4:25).

The Resurrection of Christ

Christ's resurrection from the tomb is the best-documented fact of ancient history. When He died, loving hands wrapped Him in grave clothes and buried Him, oriental fashion, in a cave. Pilate and the Jews set a Roman guard at the tomb to make sure the disciples did not steal His body. In spite of these safeguards, on the first day of the week (Sunday) the cave was found open and empty. Before He ascended to heaven, Jesus appeared alive to Mary Magdalene, other women, Peter, two disciples at Emmaus, the ten at Jerusalem, Thomas, five hundred brethren at once, his half-brother James, the seven at Galilee, and to all the apostles. He also appeared to Paul from heaven. Read John 20:16, 26; Luke 24:10, 36; and 1 Corinthians 15:5-8.

His resurrection body was in a glorified state, but it was actually the same body as before His death. His wounds were visible. He ate and talked with His disciples, and asked them to touch Him if they still doubted that it was He. On the other hand, He could become invisible at will and pass through locked doors. He never used these powers before His resurrection. The resurrection is the foundation of our faith, as the sermons in Acts show us; hence it cannot be overemphasized.

7

CHRISTOLOGY:
THE STUDY OF CHRIST
– PART 3 –

The Names of Christ

It is appropriate is this third chapter on the person and work of Christ to draw attention to His names. A large volume could be devoted to the subject of the many titles and names of Christ (which number more than 250!). We have seen how the name *Son of God* signifies Christ's eternal Sonship in the Godhead. The main meaning of the title *Son of Man* shows His true representative humanity before God. Hebrew names had much greater importance to the ancients than they do to us, but it is a worthwhile study to use a concordance and go through the Bible tracing the names, titles, and descriptive terms for Christ. Because of space limitations here, we will discuss only the three most prominent and commonly used names of our Lord in Scripture.

He is called **Lord**. This name identifies Christ's deity and authority. He is the Master, the Lord of all. Many people, sad to say, use the name quite loosely; they have no intention of submitting to Christ's lordship (John 13:13; Luke 6:46). As you read the New Testament, notice that nearly every use of the word "Lord" (when it isn't referring to a man) is referring to Jesus Christ, not to God or to the Father in particular.

His name is **Jesus**. This name, meaning "the LORD (Jehovah) is salvation," or "the salvation of the LORD," is Christ's human name and emphasizes His saviorhood. Actually, "Jesus" was a popular name for Jewish men in Christ's time. It meant the same as Joshua, of which "Jesus" is the Greek form. This name is widely used in the Gospels but not often in the Epistles without the titles "Lord" or "Christ" affixed to it. In hymns, the single of His human name is used expressively, but in general, the Son of God is worthy of His full name and title, as Paul shows us in his letters.

His title is **Christ**. This name is simply the New Testament Greek equivalent of the Old Testament Hebrew title *Messiah*, meaning "Anointed One" or "Chosen One" (compare Acts 4:26 with Psalm 2:1-2). It emphasizes our Lord's offices of Prophet, Priest, and King, as well as His Davidic lineage. Many people who use this name think of it merely as a "last name," whereas they are actually confessing in the phrase "Jesus Christ" that Jesus of Nazareth is the true Messiah. When you read "Christ Jesus" rather than "Jesus Christ" in Scripture, notice the emphasis is on His office rather than His humanity.

Truly, **Jesus,** the **Christ,** is **Lord!**

The Ascension and Present Session of Christ

In the previous two chapters we covered the person, life, and ministry of Christ chronologically from His pre-incarnate existence up through His resurrection. We will now move on to discuss His ascension and ministry in heaven.

After Jesus arose from the dead, He spent time with His disciples on different occasions over a period of forty days. He explained to them more about the Old Testament and the kingdom of God and commanded them to make disciples worldwide (Matt. 28:19-20). On the day He ascended bodily back to heaven, He commanded them to testify of Him both locally and afar; He promised to be with them at all times and to send the Holy Spirit within a few days (Acts 1:3-9).

He had come from the Father and He returned to the Father (John 16:28). He had taken on Himself the form of man and was obedient to death. God therefore highly exalted Him and gave Him a name above every name (Phil. 2:6-11). God also set Him at His own right hand in heaven and gave Him control of all things (Eph. 1:20-22).

When Jesus Christ had completed the work of atonement for sin on the cross, He cried with a loud voice, "It is finished!" (John 19:30), and then He gave up His spirit. Some people trust in their own good works to atone for their sins, but such works are forever inadequate. It is good when we gain an understanding of Christ's finished work on our behalf. It is also good to know and understand something of Christ's *unfinished* work for us. Although His sufferings are forever over, Christ is active today in heaven on our behalf. There are five words in the New Testament used to describe this present activity of Christ. Let's consider them briefly.

Jesus, our Mediator

Jesus Christ is our Mediator (1 Tim. 2:5). Job in his trouble felt the need for someone to stand between him and God (Job 9:33). Christ is the ideal Mediator, or "go-between." He has partaken of the nature of both God and man. There is only one God, only one God-Man, only one Mediator. To say we need another mediator is to say Christ is not good enough. We do not even need anyone to go between us and Christ. He is a man and He knows our hearts. Yet He is also God, and God is love.

The Law was ordained by angels in the hand of a mediator, Moses (Gal. 3:19). Christ is the Mediator of the covenant of grace. He is the Mediator of a better covenant (Heb. 8:6). He is the Mediator of the new covenant in terms of time (Heb. 9:15) and of quality (Heb. 12:24). We are brought into the benefits of this new and better covenant by grace. Christ acts as our Mediator when we come to God by faith, trusting in Christ's atoning work to save us.

Jesus, Our Priest

He is our Priest. In Old Testament times there were two heads of priestly orders, Aaron and Melchizedek. In the New Testament, Christ is a High Priest "after the order of Melchizedek" (Heb. 7:1-6) and fulfills also the functions of the Aaronic priesthood. He is superior to both Aaron and Melchizedek. Aaron and all his sons died; Christ is a High Priest forever. He is the only one called the Great High Priest (Heb. 4:14). (The priesthood of Christ is mentioned only in the book of Hebrews.) The chief duties of the High Priest are in connection with worship and intercession (Heb. 5:1-

2). Christ offered *Himself* as a perfect sacrifice acceptable to God (Heb. 10:12). As our High Priest, Christ leads our worship and makes our praise acceptable to God (Heb. 10:19-22). As Priest, because "He Himself has suffered, being tempted [tested], He is able to aid those who are tempted" (Heb. 2:18). And "He is able to save to the uttermost those who come to God through Him, since He always lives to make intercession for them" (Heb. 7:25) "according to the power of an endless life" (Heb. 7:16).

God had prescribed in the Mosaic law that the high priest would wear special, holy garments with precious stones on the shoulders and breast. On these stones were engraved the names of the twelve tribes of Israel. This was a picture of Christ as our High Priest praying for His own people and keeping them in the place of blessing (near His heart).

Jesus, Our Advocate

Jesus is our Advocate. Christ as Mediator brings sinners to God. As Priest, He keeps believers in the place of blessing. But if we fall into sin we need Christ the Advocate. "My little children, these things I write to you, so that you may not sin. And if anyone sins, we have an Advocate with the Father, Jesus Christ the righteous" (1 John 2:1). From this verse we learn two things: God's *purpose* and God's *provision*. His purpose is that I should not sin at all. But we must not deceive ourselves by thinking that we actually are sinless or perfect. When we sin, we are glad for God's provision of an adequate Advocate, Jesus Christ the righteous.

Just as a lawyer or counselor seeks to help a person in time of need, so Christ acts to restore the sinning believer to fellowship with God. Some people erroneously suppose that when we believers sin, we lose our eternal life. It is equally unscriptural to think that we can go on in sin without the Father's intervention in His disciplinary role. This same word "Advocate" (Greek, *Paraclete*) is used of the Holy Spirit and is translated "Comforter" or "Helper" in John 14:16, 26; 15:26; and 16:7. This gives another meaning to the present work of Christ. It also shows that the work of Christ and the work of the Spirit are closely related. Meditate on that.

In contrast to the work of Christ as Advocate for His saints, Satan is called the "accuser of the brethren" (Rev. 12:10). More of the work of Satan will be studied under Angelology.

Jesus, Our Shepherd

In 1 Peter 2:25 we read two other titles of Christ. First, He is our Shepherd. As the "good Shepherd," Jesus laid down His life for the sheep (John 10:11). This is past. As to the future, He is described as "the chief Shepherd" in 1 Peter 5:4, promising to reward those who faithfully serve as His under-shepherds when He appears in glory. From Hebrews 13:20-21 we can glean that it was in the power of His blood that Jesus as our "great Shepherd" ratified the new covenant to bring us into God's fold, and it is "through Christ"—through His present power as a Shepherd to feed, guide, and protect—that God channels His equipping power to "make us complete in every good work."

Jesus, Our Bishop

We read also in 1 Peter 2:25 that Christ is our Bishop. This word means "overseer" and refers to Christ as the Guardian or Superintendent of individual believers and churches. He has the right as Lord to require devoted service to Himself. He calls to task those who are careless. In Revelation 2 and 3 He knows what is going on in the seven churches. He promises rewards for faithful service even now and still greater rewards at His judgment seat. On the other hand, He is ready to remove the lamp (as a beacon of righteousness and "gospel light") of a backslidden church if it does not repent (Rev. 2:5).

In summary, let's remind ourselves that the Lord Jesus Christ now has both a human and a divine nature. He is only one personality, however—finite minds cannot plumb the depths of the God-man, but this should not surprise us. A good rule to remember when thinking about this deep subject is this: Do not divide Christ's person(ality) or confuse His two natures. The glorious truth that should strike us with awe is this: There is a Man in the glory at God's right hand—a sympathetic High Priest who knows what it is like to go through this sinful world and be misunderstood by unbelievers. Could anything be more encouraging to weak mortals such as us?

Let us now move on chronologically to consider the doctrine of Christ's second coming to earth.

The Second Coming and Glory of Christ

We have observed that the Old Testament promised a coming Messiah: Prophet, Priest, and King. When Christ was here on earth, He revealed the mind of God as Prophet (Heb. 1:1-2). Now in heaven, He intercedes for us as Priest. Soon He will return as King.

No account of Christ would be complete without reference to His coming back in glory. He came first of all in humility and was subject to the rejection, abuse, and dishonor of men. God has glorified Christ in heaven, the center of the universe; it is an essential part of God's plan that Christ should be honored right here in this world where He was rejected. When He comes again, every knee will bow to Him.

Christ is called *King* with respect to Israel rather than the church, of which He is the *Bridegroom*. Putting together relevant passages in the Old and New Testaments, we learn God's mind for the future. First, Christ will come to the clouds and receive His beloved church to Himself. This will be followed by the judgment seat of Christ and the marriage supper of the Lamb. With the church removed from this world there will at first be "progress" and prosperity for Jew and Gentile, but when God's wrath is poured forth, all this will change to the great tribulation.

One day, Christ will come in power and appear in this world. He will separate true believers from those who reject God. The rejectors will go to their doom, but believers will repopulate the earth during a time of unprecedented blessing, when Christ reigns as King. This will last for one thousand years and therefore is called the *millennium*. Satan will be restrained during this period, but at the end of it he will be released again for a short time. He will succeed in banding together the rebels of mankind in the hope of throwing off God's control. This will be met by the destruction of all who rebel be followed by the judgment of the lost dead at the great white throne. After this, heaven and earth will pass away and God will create new heavens and a new earth (1 Thess. 4:13-17; Revelation 20 and 21).

God's plan for the future is to glorify His Son. These topics will be studied in detail with the appropriate Scriptures in the final chapter of *Bible Doctrine Part 2* under Eschatology. For the present we can praise God for His wonderful provision for us in Christ through His past and present work and for the glorious future which lies before us.

8

PNEUMATOLOGY:
THE STUDY OF THE HOLY SPIRIT

Many people misunderstand the nature of the Holy Spirit; they regard Him mostly as a mysterious influence rather than a real, living personality. Let us begin our study of the person of the Holy Spirit by considering the attributes or characteristics of His personality in general.

The Person of the Holy Spirit

We might define a "person" as one who can speak, act, and express himself. In Acts 10:19-20, the Holy Spirit speaks—He says, "I have sent"; in Acts 13:2 He says, "I have called." In Revelation 2 and 3 we read seven times of what "The Spirit *says* to the churches . . ."

A person has a will of his own. So has the Holy Spirit (1 Cor. 12:11). He strives with men (Gen. 6:3). He guides us as sons of God (Rom. 8:14). A person has feelings. The Holy Spirit may be vexed (Isa. 63:10), grieved (Eph. 4:30), or insulted (Heb. 10:29). A person has intelligence; the Holy Spirit has a mind (Rom. 8:27). He searches the deep things of God and He knows the mind of God (1 Cor. 2:10-11).

> *The Holy Spirit is a person. We should never refer to Him as "it."*

A mere influence or force has no will, mind, or feelings, nor can it speak of itself as "I." The Holy Spirit is a person. We should never refer to Him as "it." (The Holy Spirit is referred to as "it" in some passages of the Bible, but only because *pneuma*, the Greek word for both "wind" and "spirit," is in the neuter gender and thus requires the neuter pronoun "it." In some passages, John 14:26, for example, the writer actually violates strict grammar by using "He" in order to stress the personality of God the Holy Spirit.)

The Deity of the Holy Spirit

In the Bible, angels are called spirits, and some of them are holy spirits. It is evident from Scripture, however, that *the* Holy Spirit has the attributes of God. The very words "Holy Spirit" (Luke 11:13) teach us that He is *Spirit* and He is *holy,* two of the divine attributes. He is *eternal* (Heb. 9:14). Every creature, every angel, has a beginning; only God is eternal. He is *sovereign,* linked in an equal way with God the Father and God the Son. Thus baptisms are carried out in the name of the Father, the Son, and the Holy Spirit (Matt. 28:19). Paul pronounced a blessing on the Corinthian saints from the triune God (2 Cor. 13:14). It would be very wrong to link up a creature as equal with God.

Putting together verses about the Holy Spirit, we can only conclude that He is co-equal with the Father and the Son.

Verses could be quoted which *seem* to suggest that the Holy Spirit is superior or inferior to the Father or the Son. For example, the Spirit proceeds from the Father and is sent by the Son (John 15:26; 16:7). In studying any subject of Scripture it is necessary to compare all verses which have a bearing on the matter. Putting together verses about the Holy Spirit, we can only conclude that He is co-equal with the Father and the Son.

He is *omnipotent.* As well as His role in creation (Gen. 1:2), it was in the power of the Spirit that Christ performed His miracles, and regeneration is the work of the Holy Spirit. He is *omniscient.* He knows the deep things of God (1 Cor. 2:10). He is *omnipresent.* In Psalm 139:7-10 we see that it is impossible to escape from the Spirit of God. He is *righteous.* He reproves the world of sin, righteousness, and judgment (John 16:8-11). He is *gracious.* He is called the Spirit of grace (Heb. 10:29). His love is brought out in Romans 15:30.

Two other attributes of God are *self-revelation* and *self-consistency.* All we know about God is revealed through the Spirit. He is called the "Spirit of truth" (John 14:17). He does reveal Himself through Scripture, but His main work is to glorify Christ (John 16:13-14). As to self-consistency, the Spirit never changes. The expression "seven Spirits of God" (Rev. 3:1) refers to the fullness and omnipresence of the Spirit. Neither this passage nor the one in Isaiah 11:2 teach that there are many divine spirits or that the Holy Spirit might act inconsistently with Himself, or with God the Father or God the Son.

The words of God in the Old Testament are often said to be the words of the Holy Spirit when quoted in the New Testament. For example, in Isaiah 6:9-10, the prophet heard the words of Jehovah, but the apostle Paul, in Acts 28:25-27, says the Holy Spirit spoke. In Jeremiah 31:31 Jehovah promises to make a new covenant with the house of Israel; in Hebrews 10:15-17 these words are said to be spoken by the Holy Spirit.

Finally—and conclusively—the Spirit is explicitly called God: in Acts 5:3-4, Peter states that Ananias, in lying to the Holy Spirit, actually lied to God.

We will now consider the works of the Holy Spirit. They all prove that He is deity, equal in every way with the Father and the Son. The Bible teaches that the Spirit of God is truly and fully God Himself.

The Work of the Holy Spirit

There is one God but He works in many different ways. Some phases of God's activities are attributed to the Father, others to the Son, still others to the Holy Spirit. There is also some overlap, whereby the same activity is attributed to the Father and the Son, or to Christ and the Spirit. This simply

> The Holy Spirit never acts contrary to the Father or the Son.

emphasizes the unity of the Godhead. The Holy Spirit never acts contrary to the Father or the Son. We list here eight areas of activity especially mentioned in connection with the Holy Spirit.

Creation

Creation is the Spirit's work in relation to the universe. While all things were created by the Son, the Spirit is referred to in regard to the creation of man (Job 33:4) and animals (Ps. 104:30). According to Job 26:13, "By His Spirit He [God] adorned the heavens" (Job 26:13) and formed the earth (Gen. 1:2).

Inspiration and Illumination

This is the Spirit's work in relation to Scripture. The grand theme of the Bible is Christ, but its inspiration is particularly by the Holy Spirit (2 Pet. 1:21). See also 2 Samuel 23:2-3; Acts 1:16; 28:25; John 14:26; 16:13; 1 Corinthians 2:10; and 1 Timothy 4:1. This subject has been dealt with more fully under Bibliology. For the believer today, the Holy Spirit acts as Illuminator of the Scripture—that is, when He makes the text clear, the believer receives the benefit of His once-for-all inspiration of it.

> The Holy Spirit acts as Illuminator of the Scripture—the believer receives the benefit of His once-for-all inspiration of it.

Incarnation

The incarnation is the Spirit's work in relation to Christ. The close connection between the Son of God and the Spirit of God is further seen in studying the experience of Christ on earth. The Holy Spirit is even called the "Spirit of Christ" in Romans 8:9. Seven ministries of the Spirit with reference to Christ might be mentioned.

1. The conception of Jesus within the Virgin Mary (Matt. 1:18; Luke 1:35)

2. The anointing of Christ after His baptism by coming on Him and abiding on Him. This act fulfilled Old Testament prophecies and proved to John the Baptist and others that Jesus was the true Messiah and was approved by God (Matt. 3:16; Mark 1:10; Luke 3:22). There was no limit to the Spirit's activity through Christ (John 3:34).

3. The Spirit led Christ into the wilderness to be tempted by Satan (Matt. 4:1; Mark 1:12; Luke 4:1).

4. After His victory over Satan, Christ entered into three years of intense activity. On many occasions He healed the sick and preached God's word. These services were performed in the power of the Holy Spirit (Luke 4:14, 18; Matt. 12:28). The Son of God in incarnation retained His omnipotence but lived the life which His Father had ordained for Him in the power of the Holy Spirit. He did not act on His own initiative or in His own power.

5. The Lord Jesus said He had authority to lay down His life and to take it again (John 10:18). Yet it was through the eternal Spirit that Christ offered Himself without spot to God (Heb. 9:14).

6. Although Christ had authority to take His life again after laying it down, in actual fact, God raised up Christ from the dead, according to Acts 2:28 and Romans 4:25. First Peter 3:18 records He was "made alive" by the Spirit.

7. The Spirit inspires the bride to yearn for Christ's return (Rev. 22:17).

Conviction

Conviction is the Spirit's work in relation to the world. He convicts the world of sin, of righteousness, and of judgment (John 16:8-11). It is only as the Spirit works that we can hope to see people brought under conviction. This involves two limitations. Since God has given man the right of free choice, He will never go back on this or force man against his will. So the divine Spirit is "limited" in a sense by man's stubborn heart. Some people resist the Holy Spirit (Acts 7:51), or insult the Spirit of grace (Heb. 10:29). On the other hand, the Spirit limits and restrains the senseless opposition and rebellion of man. He will continue to restrain until taken from this world in the special way that He is now present in the church. As the omnipresent God, He can never be literally "taken out of the way" (2 Thess. 2:7).

Regeneration

This is the Spirit's work in relation to a person who repents. By a wonderful act of the Spirit, the life of God is imparted to everyone who receives Christ, who believes on His name (John 1:12-13; 3:5-6). Although unaware of what has transpired, the individual is at that moment born again. Once eternal life is received, it cannot be lost.

———— ✍ ————

By a wonderful act of the Spirit, the life of God is imparted to everyone who receives Christ.

———— ✍ ————

Sanctification

This is the Spirit's work in relation to the believer. This topic is developed more fully in the lessons on Soteriology in the second part of this ECS course but also belongs here as a fundamental activity of the Holy Spirit. When a person is born again, he is sanctified, set apart for God. This happens only once, but sanctification is also a daily process for the rest of one's life. Both positional and practical sanctification are the work of the Holy Spirit (1 Pet. 1:2). Daily cleansing is also the work of Christ (Eph. 5:26). To accomplish this work, the Holy Spirit indwells each believer permanently (1 John 2:27), produces fruit in the life (Gal. 5:22), and desires to fill each one (Eph. 5:18). It is possible for a true child of God to hinder the Spirit's work. The Scripture warns against grieving the Spirit (Eph. 4:30) and quenching the Spirit (1 Thess. 5:19).

Seal, Guarantee, Baptism

Three other terms are used to describe the Holy Spirit's relationship to the believer: seal, guarantee, and baptism. The Holy Spirit within us is the *seal* that we are the property of God (Eph. 1:13). He is also the *guarantee,* or pledge, of our inheritance—that is, He assures us that we are sons of God (Eph. 1:14). At the moment of our conversion to Christ we become members of His body by virtue of the once-for-all *baptism* of the Holy Spirit on the day of Pentecost (see 1 Cor. 12:13). This historic baptism took place for the express purpose of uniting *all* believers into one harmonious organism—the body of Christ.

Each of these three terms describes an unconditional blessing imparted by the Holy Spirit to every believer: that is, we as believers do not receive any of these blessings on the basis of our own worthiness, efforts, prayers, etc. Rather, God graciously gives these blessings to each of us in order to strengthen and encourage us from the very outset of our Christian lives. He does expect us to thank Him for them.

Filling of the Spirit

Sometimes the filling of the Holy Spirit is confused with His baptizing. Unlike the baptism, which becomes every believer's unconditional blessing at the moment of his conversion, the filling of the Holy Spirit is conditional. It is dependent (among other things) on a believer's daily confession of every known sin and his complete yieldedness to Father, Son, and Holy Spirit. Paul tells us in 1 Corinthians 12:13 that we (believers) are all baptized by one Spirit into one body, but he exhorts us in Ephesians 5:18 to be filled (literally, "be being filled") with the Spirit, producing, among other things, the fruit of the Spirit (Gal. 5:22-23). The Spirit of God longs that we yield to His operating in us daily. Let us give Him opportunity to do so!

> ———— ✍ ————
>
> **The Spirit of God longs that we yield to His operating in us daily. Let us give Him opportunity to do so!**
>
> ———— ✍ ————

In the Old Testament, the Holy Spirit came upon certain individuals in a temporary way for special work (Ex. 28:3; Num. 27:18; 1 Sam. 16:13). He could also work on and through an ungodly man, such as Balaam (Num. 24:2). He departed from Saul (1 Sam. 16:14), and even the inspired psalmist in time of sin prayed that the Holy Spirit might not be taken from him (Ps. 51:11). The Lord Jesus described the difference between the Old and New Testament dispensations by saying of the Holy Spirit, "He dwells *with* you and *will be in* you" (John 14:17, emphasis added).

For further study the student would do well to consider the symbols of the Holy Spirit used in Scripture, those of oil, water, wind, fire, and dove. The ECS course *The Holy Spirit at Work* is a good resource. We should remember that when we learn the doctrine of the Holy Spirit, we become responsible to yield to His power and control over our lives.

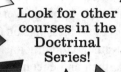

Look for other courses in the Doctrinal Series!

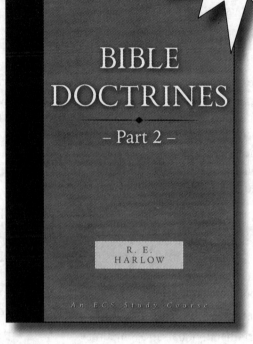

DOCTRINAL SE

BIBLE DOCTRINES
– Part 2 –

R. E. HARLOW

An ECS Study Course

G reat job completing *Bible Doctrines – Part 1.* You've learned about the Bible, God, Jesus Christ, and the Holy Spirit. But don't stop studying . . . there's still more to learn.

Bible Doctrines – Part 2 will guide you through a topical study of the other major teachings of Scripture, referencing many relevant verses relating to each doctrine. With an open Bible and an open heart, you will indeed profit from learning what the Scripture teaches about angels, man, sin, salvation, the church, and future events. So go ahead, get started today.

Call or go online for more information:
563-585-2070 or www.ecsministries.org